Adored

A Collection of Poetry

By

HA Blackwood

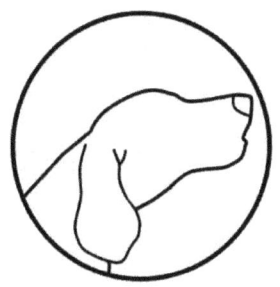

Baying Hound Media

USA

Disclaimers and Copyright

This book is a work of fiction. Names, characters, places, and incidents are the product of the author's imagination and are used fictitiously. Any resemblance to actual persons, living or dead, locales, or events—no matter how much it seems like it directed at you—is purely coincidental.

This book is protected under the copyright laws of the United States of America. Any reproduction or other unauthorized use of the material or artwork herein is prohibited under penalty of law without the express written permission of the author or publisher.

Adored

A Collection of Poetry

Copyright © 2021 by HA Blackwood
All rights reserved.
Published by Baying Hound Media
Edited by Baying Hound Media
ISBN: 978-1-955670-02-9

Introduction

Before you get into this book, you should understand that I've never considered myself to be a poet. I fell into poetry quite by accident via my twitter account. I'm involved in what you can call Dirty Twitter – a group of kinky, dirty minded perverts who share (or over share, depending on your viewpoint) their predilections. They are some of the kindest, least judgmental people I've had the good fortune to be associated with and oh my god, are they fun. One of the things many of us engage in are themes picture days - #ManThighMonday, #TittyTuesday, #HumpDay, etc, etc, where we post pictures that vary from tame to risqué to downright graphic. It's all in good fun and to be honest there are times where I've been absolutely amazed at the creativity deployed in these themes.

Like all online communities, however, there are the bottom dwellers. The men (mostly) who can't formulate a thought without being crass or rude. When a woman posts a themed picture dressed provocatively with a string of pearls as the centerpiece of the photo, these cretins comment things like "Nice tits!" or "I'll give you a pearl necklace."

That's how I found my way into poetry. I started commenting a few lines that highlighted the theme of the photo without overtly focusing on the body of the woman in the photo in question. I found they liked it – and some were actually waiting for me to post one about them on one of their tweets. I kept this up for a few weeks, but I have to tell you, trying to come up with a unique bit of prose for several women each day there's a themed photo day (which is every day ending in a Y) is tough mentally, and eventually I stopped doing it, just dropping one in periodically when the mood struck me, or a picture was particularly moving.

So, my poetry moved into its current phase. I started doing poetry in the style of subtweets. A subtweet, if you don't know, is a tweet sent to a specific person, but that person is not named. An effective subtweet will be read by multiple people who think it applies to them, and they vary from pathetic (usually from a man who isn't getting what he wants from a woman, in my experience) to demeaning to clever.

> PATHETIC: "I CAN'T KEEP PUTTING MYSELF OUT THERE. IT DOESN'T DO ANYTHING BUT CAUSE HURT. I'M AN IDIOT."

That's a real subtweet from a psycho who was stalking a woman who wanted nothing to do with him, and his tweets actually became more threatening, which can be scary. As an aside – guys, do better. This is red flag behavior and any woman who sees this is going to run far, far away from you. Your parade of misery via subtweet is going to be a self-fulfilling prophesy. You'll be sad, and bitter and lonely on Dirty Twitter, because not only is your timeline unattractive, but the lovely women you're scaring away tend to talk to each other. You'll end up having to spend your evenings with your wife, for god's sake. But I digress.

Demeaning subtweets are typically deployed against men like the one above, or against 'reply guys' (a whole topic unto itself I'm not going to get into here).

> DEMEANING: "WELL WELL WELL IF IT ISN'T THE DM SLIDE OF YOUR OWN UNCONTROLLED FLIRTING."

The recipient of the demeaning subtweet should feel appropriately shamed, and if they don't, at least the person sending the tweet is getting a good laugh at their expense.

> CLEVER: "THE WAY YOU ROMANCE MY HEART LEAVES ME BREATHLESS."
>
> "YOUR IMPERFECTIONS ARE WHAT MAKE YOU UNIQUE."
>
> "I WANT YOU TO BEGIN AND END MY EVERY MEMORY."

These are all designed so that just about anyone could think it's about them, or they can identify with the sentiment. Yes, my imperfections DO make me unique! I would LOVE to be the alpha and omega to all your memories!

The clever subtweet leaves people feeling good, uplifted, romantic, horny, appreciated. Based on the number of these types of tweets I see, and the frequency with which they come from the same people, I suspect these clever subtweets are being written more for the effect they have, and not to direct a message to a particular person; but you can't tell for sure, and that's part of what makes them so great.

That leads me to my current poetry theme. I've been writing fantastical, romantic, grandiose poems in subtweet fashion, not every night, but often enough. Rather than five or six poems a day to five or six women, I write one poem to ALL the women of Twitter. Or men – I really don't mind if they imagine I'm speaking to them. It's the beauty of the subtweet – it can apply to anyone! People really seem to like them, as I get a lot of feedback and retweets where people either identify with or simply feel moved by the sentiments expressed.

Are my poems written about or inspired by a specific person? Maybe. Maybe not. Telling you would strip them of some of their magic. I will tell you that they hit me on their own schedule. A rainstorm brings me an idea. The moon shining through a window sends me a message. A vision when I close my eyes sends me in a sensual direction. Maybe there's a muse in all of this. Maybe she reaches out and touches me, providing inspiration. If there is, she knows it when she sees these poems on my timeline. Or maybe she doesn't. That's the mystery of the subtweet. You never know.

    Unless you do.

Stardust

She's made of stardust
I am the sea
I reflect the light
She twinkles at me

Celestial beauty
Wraps me in love
If I am the fingers
She is my glove

As vast as the ocean
More so the sky
She's made of stardust
And now so am I

Always

You are my favorite song
With music that never ends.
A poem that never stops rhyming.
A sunset that goes on and on
Keeping lit forever the fire in my heart.
You are my always

Gravity

My heart in your hands
Beats a tune only for you

Your mind creates for me a world
Into which I want to disappear

Your soul wrapped around mine
Ignites a thousand stars
In a thousand galaxies

And uses their gravity
To ensure nothing can pull us apart

Pearls

Pearls come from the sea

Tiny treasures made for thee

Like your dreams, each one unique

Like a woman whose heart you seek

Like red, red lips that make knees weak

Pearls come from the sea

Tiny treasures made for me

Perfection

You have scars, physical and mental
You're fractured, broken in places

You've been in the darkness and brought some of it out with you
But you're not an object to be fixed, you're a goddess to be loved

Your struggles are a part of you
And you're perfect just the way you are

One

Out of all the hours
In all the days
In all the weeks
In all my years
My life was redefined
By just one moment
With you

Jeans

Fresh air, green grass, and a good pair of blue jeans
Holding hands, smiles and laughs, that means everything
Summer sky, apple pie, and the county fair
Simpler times, in my mind, your jeans take me there

Cosmos

I could cross the cosmos
and skirt the ever-expanding edge of the universe
and I would never find another being
as perfect to my eyes are you are right now

Creation

As the sun goes down,
my soul takes flight,
meeting yours
to dance across the cosmos
while we slumber.

Their celebration
casts off sparks
that become stars
in faraway galaxies,
so that long after we're gone,
our love will continue
to make the universe glow

Distance

Delicate fingers touch places my lips have been

With a smile of remembrance upon her face

I yearn to once again taste her porcelain skin

As I long to return to her loving embrace

Regret

The only regrets I have in life
Are all the moments I lost
Before I met your perfect soul

Most

Of all the things I love about you
        Your mind
        Your swagger
        Your laughter
        Your behind
        Your face
        Your lips
        Your chest
        Your grace
        Your arms
        Your legs
        Your smile
        Your charm
        And on and on
        And on and on
        And on
The thing I love the most
        Is you

Safe

Late at night
When I can't sleep
And dark thoughts
Around edges creep
When nightmares come
In sleep so still
With torment's goal
And demon's will
I reach my hand
To find you there
Radiant face
Flowing hair
My rising sun
No dark can face
My love in you
Is my safe space

Shieldmaiden

You're my shieldmaiden
You're my china doll
So fierce in battle
So fragile when you fall

No one I'd rather enter battle with
No one I'd rather hold tight
No better partner in life
No better lover at night

Always it's you and me
Always my partner in crime
Our life is full of wonder
Our love is for all time

Wisdom

If she gives you her time, use it wisely.
It's the greatest gift she can give you
For it can't be replaced if you waste it

Raindrops

Rain cascades from heavy, sodden clouds
I see you in the violent sky
Hear you in the roaring storm
Feel you in the rattling wind

Each drop is a deposit on a kiss
Each thunderclap an embrace
Each bolt of lightning a moment of bliss

Bringing me closer to heaven
Closer to you

Home

In the dark and cold depth of night
When sleep flees, replaced with fear
She thinks of me, her shining light
She holds my heart and keeps me near

I feel her touch from far away
I caress her cheek and kiss her tear
I hold her tight 'til break of day
I gave my heart with purpose clear

To show my love is hers alone
Always my heart is her safe home

Cosmos

Come lay next to me and hold my hand
You can show me all the stars you're made of
And we'll count them until dawn

Lifetimes

Lost
In your eyes
Sapphire blue galaxies
We spend a lifetime
Living
Loving
Having adventures
Holding
Hugging
Carnal pleasures
Aging
Adoring
A lifetime lived
When I'm lost
In your eyes

Adored

Captured

Your sapphire blue eyes lured me in
I swam across them only to get entangled
In your strawberry lips
I devoured them only to find
Your mind was a net cast wide
Teaching me your language
While your soul enveloped me
Wrapping me in a warm glow
And making me yours

Close

There's no distance across which I cannot love you.
No separation that can keep me from your mind, and from there, your body.
When souls mesh, distance disappears.

Desire

A sigh in the night
I feel you
A scent of desire
I breathe you in
A fluttering heart
I need you
A hitch in your breath
We begin
A shuddering gasp
I claim you
A lover's embrace
Skin to skin
A moment to breathe
I explore you
A need unspoken
We start again

Bespoke

My heart is an undying forge
Lit by your love and stoked by your breath
With it I will build for you a world
Befitting your beautiful soul

Rulers

The ocean's fury is unmatched on earth
Yet it is powerless against the pull of the moon

I am the ocean, roiling, boiling, and raging
She is my moon, her gravity tames my tides

I reflect her beauty, while she bends me to her will
And thus, together, we rule the world

Warrior

She's a warrior. She's been wounded, scarred
Fight for her. She'll reward you.
Support her. She'll praise you.
Love her. She'll open her heart

She's a warrior. She's been wounded, scarred.
Hurt her. Neglect her. Wound her.
She's a warrior. She'll cut you down

Alternatives

If only I'd met you sooner
If only we had that time
If only years and years ago
I got to make you mine

We wouldn't have our magic
We wouldn't have our night
When it comes to timing
It turns out fate is right

Apace

Lay against me, your arm over me, your head on my chest.
Your steady breathing stills my raging mind, calming my heart.
My heart, your breath, pacing each other.
Pulling us toward slumber
Pulling us toward peace

Love

Love is
Unpredictable
It won't be forced
Love is
Undeniable
It can't be stopped
Love is
Uncontrollable
It isn't up to you
Love is
Unconditional
It doesn't bargain
Love is
Perfect with you

Finally

I see your face in the sky above
Mesmerizing, radiant, aglow
You bring me peace like the purest dove
A feeling I never thought I'd know
You fit my life like a velvet glove
And see sides of me I never show
I finally get this thing called love
It just took your heart for me to know

Occupied

You occupy a piece of every thought I have
So that I'm thinking of you
Even when I'm not

Soaring

Love letters
Written on my soul
Your handwriting
Telling our story
Where we are
Where we've been
Where we'll be
Always happy
Together forever
Bound by love
But flying free

Grateful

The days are long
The road is hard
But at the end is you
Waiting
Giving me the gift of your time
Which makes me grateful
The days are long

Consumed

Kiss her hard, and deep
Without saying a word
Tell her how much you want her
How much you NEED her
Let her know she ignites your blood
And consumes your mind
The way you're going to consume her body
And set fire to her soul
Tell her with a kiss

Yours

My veins are filled with fire for you
Molten desire burning me through
My mind the place where you reside
You've never left once you came inside
My heart it beats just for you
90,000 times before each day's through
In my arms, you I'll keep
From morning's rise to evening's sleep
From the day we met, 'til the very end
I'm your lover, partner, mate
And friend

Untamed

I watched in awe
As you rode untamed
Through the world
Enchanted
Enamored
You bade me
Join you
Emboldened
Embraced
We take our wild
And ride through the world
Eclectic
Ecstatic
I became We
And nothing will ever
Be the same again

Needed

I need you.
I need you more than my next breath.
For without you, what's the point of breathing?

I need you more than my next heartbeat.
For without you, what good is my heart?

I need you more than my soul.
For what good is eternity without you at my side?

I
Need
You

Beauty

Every time I see you
Every day
Every moment
With every struggle
And every win
You're the most beautiful
You've ever been
Every moment I love you
You eclipse yourself
A brilliant moon
Glowing ever brighter
Pulling me in
Showing the world
The woman within

More

Deeper
Our love

Stronger
Our bond

Faster
My heart beats

Closer
You feel

Brighter
Your smile

Sweeter
Our time

Tighter
Our bodies press

Grateful
We're real

Same

When her gaze lands on me
My heart beats faster
My breathing quickens
I grow butterflies in my stomach too

I ask her how she's doing
Her pupils dilate as she takes my hand
Her breath catches in her throat

"Oh, my darling," comes the answer
"I'm doing the same as you."

Incremental

Piece by piece
We learned each other
Magnets clicked
And we fell

Kiss by kiss
We grew together
Love sprouted
Hearts swelled

Day by day
We felt forever
Each moment
A story to tell

Side by side
We claim the other
For you are mine
And I'm yours as well

Unspoken

I live for the quiet moments
Where we just let our fingers
Explore and feel each other's
Curves, angles, and valleys

No need to speak
For nothing needs said
We exist in a timeless moment
Of harmony and peace
Of love and lust
Of awe and trust

And that is everything

Ordained

Fate brought us together
At the right place and time
A touch light as a feather
A love that always rhymes

Across the void of space
A connection deep and real
A thread holds us in place
A bond that we can feel

It can't be quite explained
The link between our minds
But destiny ordained
This love of yours and mine

Rescued

I am lost in your curves
Forgetting the world exists
I am found in your touch
Exciting and electric
I am consumed by your mind
Complex and mysterious
I am saved by your heart
Loving and pure

Unprepared

I wasn't prepared for you
The blinding light of your mind
The hurricane of your passion
The overwhelming intensity of your beauty
And the loving fury with which you consumed me
I wasn't prepared for any of it
And I couldn't be happier

Changes

I opened my
Heart
Mind
Soul
To you
And that changed everything.

When you opened yours
To me
Everything changed again

And I learned what it meant
To feel joy

Another

The morning sun signals a new day
Another chance to hold you
Another chance to touch my lips
To your skin
Another chance to mold you
To the curves of my body as we cling
To each other's sin
Another chance to smile
For never shall we part
The morning sun signals a new day
In which to give you my heart

Thousands

Your eyes tell the tale
Of the thousand lives you've lived
A thousand times you've claimed my love
With a thousand hearts to give
A thousand times you've found me
A thousand times we fell
A look into our future
A thousand more as well
Forever will our souls be merged
With help from Fate above
Forever will we be so matched
Bound by eternal love

Sword

You didn't need rescued
You needed a sword in your hand
And one by your side
Held by someone who will always fight
Alongside you
Who will always fight
For you
And will give their everything
To ensure you get your chance
To slay the dragon

Miracles

You're the miracle I never knew I needed.

I'm the miracle you didn't think you deserved.

But our souls knew all along

Patiently waiting for us to be ready

Before showing us what life can be

Soulsmate

I've given you forever
Long before we met
For our love is eternal
Our fated path is set

In each life it varies
When our bodies meet
But our souls are tied together
Our bond of love complete

Moonrise

I feel your touch in the setting sun
I hear your heart beat in the rising moon
A million moments together we've run
A million times you've made me swoon

In the rising sun I see your face
The breaking dawn reveals your smile
Our loves journey has shown your grace
Our love grows each passing mile

You feel my touch in the setting sun
The day's adventure done too soon
You whisper sweetly that I'm the one
Whose heart you hear in the rising moon

Unconditional

I love you when you're up
I love you when you're down
I love you when you're far away
Or just across our town

I love you when you're smiling
I love you when you're blue
I love you when you're fighting mad
And no matter what you do

I love you without condition
I love you through and through
There's nothing in heaven or earth
That can stop my love for you

Visions

Your eyes are twin galaxies
Containing a thousand suns
Your smile a shining prophesy
From which I'll never run

Your kiss is soft as a feather
From the whitest dove
Your soul a soothing blanket
Wrapping me in your love

Hunted

I saw that look
And my defenses fell
You set the hook
I was under your spell

You led me away
As you often do
You caught your prey
Or did I catch you?

Magic

You're magical to me
You live in each heartbeat
You're part of each thought
You're in all that I see

With just a word or two
You can calm all my storms
I'm incredibly blessed
By the magic that is you

Claimed

Your eyes
Claim my gaze
Pulling me in
With their gravity

Your hips
Claim my hands
Tracing your curves
With mad desire

Your hands
Claim my body
Wandering at will
Seizing your prize

Your heart
Claims my love
Lighting a fire
For all to see

Nature

Words are inadequate to express
The range of emotions brought out of me
When faced with images of your beauty
No sonnet, no soliloquy can capture you
You are the sunrise
The blood moon
The nighttime sky
You are nature
You are all things
And I live in perpetual awe of you

You

You
Set the sun in motion
Lighting up my day

You
Mark the path ahead
Helping me find my way

You
Quiet my mind at night
Helping me to sleep

You
Opened your heart to me
And I fell in love so deep

Ethereal

She is musical
The soundtrack to my life
She is lyrical
Her words make me swoon
She is ethereal
A vision not of this world
She is magical
Because she is all these things

And she is mine

Effortless

You'd been here before
You warned me away
But you fell as hard
And wanted to stay
We're effortless, and easy
And so worth the wait
It wasn't our choice
We were matched up by fate

Needs

You didn't know how much you needed me
But once you knew me
You wondered how you lived
Without me
Without you
I can't imagine life
For once I knew you
I understood how much I needed you

Intimate

Intimacy isn't just about physical pleasure.
It's about being close, caring about the little things.
Providing comfort.
Being tender when needed
And rough when wanted.
It's paying attention to likes & dislikes.
It's innocent touches as you pass in the hall.
Intimacy is everything

Wondrous

I see your face in the morning sky
Every day like it's the first time
I breathe you deep and wonder why
It took so long to make you mine

Legendary

Sometimes I envision 100 years into the future
And people catch wind of our romance
And talk about how it inspired so much beauty

Foretold

We were always meant to be
Before there was you and I
Before there was earth and sky
Before there had formed this land
Before the universe began to expand
The gods looked down and they could see
In this time there'd be you and me

Reciprocal

Call me Baby
Make my heart beat fast
Call me Love
Give me butterflies
Give me your love
I'll give you mine
Give me your heart
And I'll give you everything

Unlocked

She carried a key all her life
Never knowing what it was for
It seemed important so she held it tight
But it never fit lock nor door
Still she kept it close to heart
Until the day she came to see
The key wasn't for a lock to start
She possessed the key to me

Gifts

I told you I would give you the world

And I will

One piece at a time

Starting with my heart

Only

Only you

Have my loyalty and trust

Only you

See me without my armor

Only you

Get the real me, unfiltered

Only you

Have my heart and soul

When it comes to my love, there is

Only you

Ambush

Your beauty is dangerous.
You ambush me with every photo
My heart beats faster
My stomach flips over
And it takes a moment to recover.
Please

Oh, please

Send another

Storytelling

I'm going to write our story on your skin
With my lips and tongue as the quill and ink
When I've covered you top to bottom, front and back
I'll return to the top and begin again

Missing

This was one of those mornings where I woke up
reaching for you
Missing your head on my chest as it was in my dreams.
I shut my eyes to the dawn, seeking a few more moments
of bliss
As your breath tickles my chest hair
And our curves fit together like two halves of a whole

Looper

If I ever end up in a time loop, just know
Especially knowing you as I do now
I'm choosing you over and over and over.
You're not perfect, but you're perfect to me
And I'll happily choose eternity with you

Beacon

When the moon goes dark
Never fear, my love
The glow from your soul
Means you're near, my love
There's no distance that
Can keep us apart
I will always find you
My shining star

Grace

When sleep has fled
And voices mute
When thoughts unbidden
Run me through
I cling to this
My strongest truth
My saving grace
Is always you

Synchrony

Your pulse echoes in my mind
Synchronizing my heart with yours
Pumping my desire through me like a drug
Making every heartbeat deliver
My need to love you
To every cell in my body

Fuel

I am the tinder box
You are the spark
Separate, we just exist
Together, we make beautiful fire

Unconditional

When I gave you my heart, it meant a few things
I'll always see the best in you, and forgive the worst
I'll celebrate the good and forget the bad
And I'll never, ever stop believing in you
I gave you my heart without conditions
So you always have a safe place to rest

Persistence

I can't carry a tune
But I'll sing for you
I can't bend a spoon
But I'll move a mountain or two
There's a lot I can't do
But I'll find a way
My heart is yours
And with you I'll stay
My love is true
And I'll show you each day

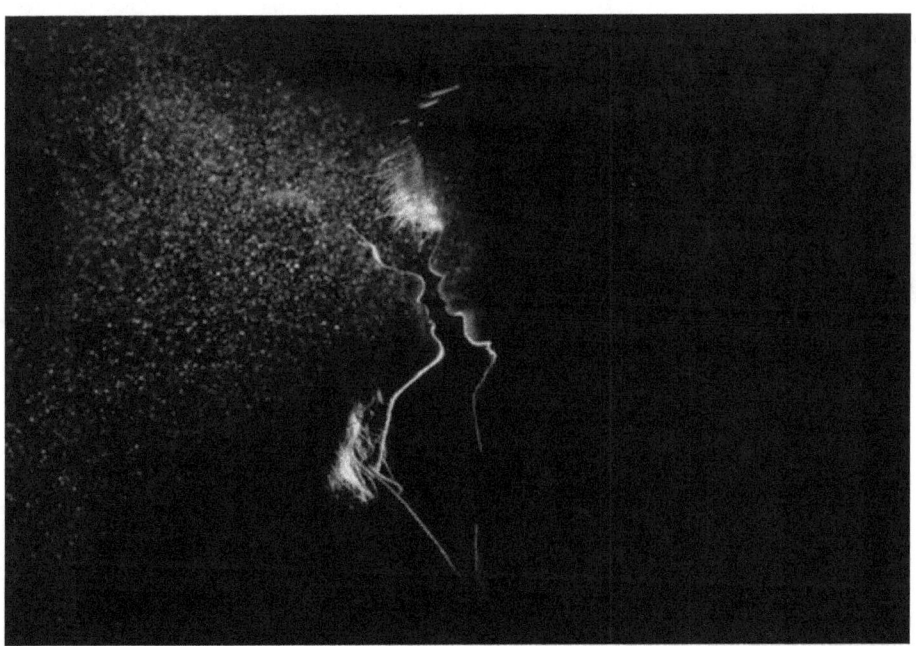

Conception

I see your face in the stars

Where the gods conceived your beauty

I hear your voice in the wind

Where they took the melody to make you sing

I feel your hand on my heart

Where you placed it when I opened myself to you

I feel your soul on mine

Where it belongs until the end of time

Content

I think of you late at night
And my soul connects with yours
Dragging me under a blanket of slumber
Leaving me with dreams of your touch
And keeping me content until morning

Senses

My eyes were open wide
But since I became yours
They're open much wider

My colors shone bright
But since you became mine
They shine so much brighter

You've heightened my senses
And expanded my world
I'm always your man
And you're forever my girl

Reminder

Have you forgotten?
I'll remind you.
You are brilliant
Drowning out the sun
You are a warrior
Slaying dragons
You are a muse
Inspiring art
You are a goddess
Worthy of worship
You are mine
Loved, vital, needed
Have you forgotten?
I'll remind you
To me
You are all things
To me
You are perfect

Voices

My name drips from your lips
Onto my skin
Hot, molten words
Running down your chin
Sending chills through me
Leaving me no choice
Everything thrills me
When wrapped in your voice
I feel your pulse quicken
When I return your name
Hearing it spoken
Thrills you the same

Untamed

She's wild
With a feral heart
To tame that heart
Is to break her spirit
And you lose the very thing
You love about her
Find your wild
Set your feral free
Run with her and find out
How great her love can be

Hands

She's not fragile
She carries the weight
Of the past
Of the present
Of the world
She makes it look easy
People forget
Sometimes she needs a hand
That she won't ask for
Because she's not fragile
Grab hold, show her
She'll have help
Carrying her future

Playwright

It's you and me
And the world's a stage
In love and free
Scripting our own page

The players in this play
They haven't a clue
At the end of the day
It's me and you

Revelation

A fated plan

A scarlet thread

A life spent waiting

A fantasy fed

At last revealed

This plan of fate

My beautiful woman

You were worth the wait

Replay

Slide under the covers
Skin to pliant skin
Two frenzied lovers
Writhing in sin
When you think it's over
We do it again and again

Biometrics

You simultaneously
Make my heart race
And take my breath away

Portfolio

What might have been
Is worthless currency

What is has value
It's an investment

In what will be
Which with you
Has value beyond measure

Savior

Wounds torn open
Spirit wrecked
On my knees
Praying for death

In your hands
My soul sings
Wounds forgotten
Bounding glee

Three words saved me
"I love you"
And oh, my darling
I love you, too

Firestarter

She sets the world on fire

With a mind full of desire

Knowing that from the start

Imagine what she does to my heart

Archery

Your words are like arrows
In your quiver
Your voice is the bow
Your aim precise
Your release deadly
My heart pierced
One shot
And I'm yours

Heaven-sent

She's my angel
Rare beauty
From the inside out
Kiss of lips
So fruity
Strawberry pout
She spreads her wings
Soaring
Passion is born
I see her halo
Held up by her horns

Inside

In my arms
You feel so right
In my eyes
You're a shining light
In my mind
You're a love so sweet
In my life
You make me complete

Be

Believe
In fate
In love

Behold
Our beauty
Our dreams

Become
One body
One soul

Belong
Together
To each other

Intertwined

Your soul
And mine
Forever entwined

Our Fate
Our minds
Always combined

Our love
All time
Shall be enshrined

Sunrise

My sun doesn't rise

Until I see her face

Morning, noon, thru long day's end

Lover, partner, truest friend

From early morning 'til night's reprise

In her arms I find my happy place

Spoken

I speak of magic
I speak of fate
A wondrous love
Our hearts create

I speak of time
A clock anew
I am forever
Bound to you

Expansion

The Universe
Must constantly expand
To make room
For our love

Courage

If I had made a different choice
I'd have never heard your perfect voice
If my nerve had failed that day
Our life unlived would've gone away
But my courage held and my heart was true
And from that day it's been me and you
We go together hand in glove
Bound forever by our fated love

Immortal

You knew me long before we met
And the moment we did, I remembered
A thousand lifetimes spent at your side
Our souls have been connected
Since the dawn of time
Instead of saying hello, you said
"I am yours, and you are mine."

Clicks

Soft lips
Finger tips
Seeking
Tasting
Searching
Wanting

Switch flips
Bag of tricks
Pulling
Rubbing
Writhing
Groaning

Firm grips
Thrusting hips
Rutting
Moaning
Growling
Owning

Needs Eclipsed
Love Transfixed
Holding
Caring
Loving
Sharing

Souls click
Recharging
Repeating

Falling

I didn't fall for you.
That implies it was a single event
The truth is, I fell
and I'm still falling

Feelings

The way I feel
When you look at me
Filled with joy
For all to see

The way you feel
When I return your gaze
Awash in bliss
Your soul ablaze

The way we feel
Our hearts are sure
A perfect fit
A love so pure

Ignition

Our thoughts and desires
Are whispered in the dark
Scamper and crawl over our skin
Each one giving off a spark
That only we can see
Igniting our passions in blazing fire
Basking in the glow of you and me

Instantaneous

One look
The world seems new
I'm filled with hope
And possibilities without end

One look
Love turns to lust
I lose all control
The beast is unleashed

One look
My heart melts
I hold you tight
And keep you safe

One look
Is all it took

She

She's my shooting star
Blazing bright
My wish come true
Every night

She's my perfect fit
Snug, and tight
She's made for me
She feels right

She's my soul's mate
My shining light
It's her I love
With all my might

Goddess

Forged in fire
Phoenix risen
Strength untold
Laser vision
Take my hand
Lover's need
Souls are bound
But spirits freed
Warrior goddess
Queen of mine
Love unlimited
For all time

Click

All the years we've been alive
All the things that we've experienced
All the people we've known
All the conversations we've had
And our combined fate hinged
On one moment
One 'click'
Everything fell into place
Our world came alive
Such is the magic of Us

Artistry

No portrait captures your beauty
The way my eye takes you in
No sculptor casts in bronze
The way you've carved my heart
You are to my love like a sinner to sin
One cannot exist without the other
For you are the artist and the art

Wit

It was your wit
That did me in

While your beauty
Distracted my eyes
With its sweet perfection

Your words, wit, and wisdom
Worked their way
Through my system

Before I knew what happened
I was yours

Direction

If the gods made an offer
Of money and fame
A superstar's life
Or leave things the same
I know without question
Just what I would do
I'll choose the path
That leads me to you

Expanded

My eyes were open wide
But since I became yours
They're open much wider

My colors shone bright
But since you became mine
They shine so much brighter

You've heightened my senses
And expanded my world
I'm always your man
And you're forever my girl

Taste

I want to taste
Joy, from your tears
Truth, from your lips
Passion, from you fingers
Lust, from your body
Love, from your heart
Life, from your soul
I want to taste
You

Choices

Your hand touches mine
Comfort in the dark
Small, tender caress
An arrow hits its mark
A stem can't choose its apple
Nor a leaf can choose its tree
But I am forever grateful, love
To your heart for choosing me

Ferocity

My love for you is fierce
I want you here and now
I'll care for and protect you
And try to make you proud
My love for you is feral
You unleash the beast in me
I'll ravish you sans mercy
And set your animal free
My love for you is endless
Unconditional too
I'll spend my life, day and night
Always loving you

Found

I find you in times of need
Your hand in mine
My worries freed

I find you when times are rough
Our touch is tender
Our defenses tough

I find you in times of sin
With devil's ease
You draw me in

I find you in times of love
Our union blessed
By gods above

For all the times that I find you
I love that you
Can find me too

Celestial

She's made of stardust, blazing through my skies
A celestial goddess, in corporeal form
Her beauty unmatched, galaxies in her eyes
She touches my soul, and I feel reborn

Forever

Ancient rhymes
Modern times

Desperate need
Wounds that bleed

Hand of Fate
Heaven's gate

Love, adore
Forevermore

Storms

You came at me like thunder
Poured over me like rain
Lit me up like lightening
I'd never be the same
Swept up in your storms
Your favorite weather, true
You blew down my defenses
And I fell in love with you

Gifts

I'll pluck a star from the sky
To put in your hair
Capture moonbeams in a jar
To light up your lair
I'll take thunder from the storm
And the shine from the sun
I'll give you the universe
Before I am done

Everything

You're the lyrics to my favorite song
You're my favorite show made extra long
You're my team with the champion's crown
You're a majestic sky as the sun goes down
You're my happiest day I wish would never end
You're my everything: my inspiration, my lover, my friend

Elemental

You're my air
When I can't breathe
You're my fire
When I need heat
You're my water
When I need a drink
You're my earth
When I plant my feet
When it comes to life
Untethered and free
You're the only element
That this man needs

Beasts

The animal in me desires

The animal in you

One look from you and he joins the fray

Bruises and bite marks abound

When you invite my beast out to play

All

All the love I have to give
All the life I have to live
All the joy I have to share
All the times my soul lay bare
All the days I long for you
All the nights you've seen me through
From the day I saw your name
I knew I'd never be the same
And I know, my love, it's true
Our time together has changed you too

Wishing

She was a shooting star
Falling to earth
I didn't need to make a wish
Because I wished for her

Relativity

Since meeting you I understand
The relativity of time
My years before were static
Waiting in an eternal line

With you, now, my days go fast
Filled with fun, exciting stuff
When it comes to loving you
A thousand years won't be enough

Reminders

I find you in the pouring rain
Thunder rumbling o'er the land
I want to laugh and dance and sing
And get soaked, hand in hand
I find you in the midday sun
Invisible rays delivering heat
Warm and dry and cozy now
Wrapped in you this can't be beat
I find you in the midnight sky
Twinkling stars and glowing moon
Sprinkling stardust o'er my heart
Love so rare it makes me swoon
No matter where I look I find
Things that remind me of you
For you, my love, are my everything
And fill my life through and through

Conspiracy

Long ago
And far away
Our souls conspired
And planned the day
That we would meet
And bond this way
Loving, happy
Forever we'd stay
Years from now
Hand in hand
Our souls will smile
About their plan
It came to pass
They knew it sure
Together forever
Our love so pure

Evolution

New Year, New Me
A phrase that should never be
We constantly evolve and adapt
Our potential for growth is untapped
The day I was born anew
Was the day that I met you

Distant

Love found me
Half a world away
From your embrace

Cruel and spiteful
Love didn't contend
That with you

Distance isn't enough
To keep our hearts apart

Names

What's in a name?
Just the thought of yours
Makes my heart beat faster
My lips tingle when it crosses them
In conversation or rapt with pleasure
Sometimes I write your name
Just to feel the butterflies
I see it cross my screen
And it steals my breath
Your name makes me feel
Alive
Excited
Peace
Love
What's in a name?
Everything

Challenges

When times are hard
Challenges need faced
And courage gathered
That's when we shine
We boost each other
Lending our strength
Locking our hands
And stiffen our spines
We fight together
Until the battle is won
If it takes a day
Or a new year chimes
I am yours
You are mine
From the day we met
Through the end of time

Fearless

When crisis reigns
And times are tough
We grab each other
And that's enough
In our arms
Or side by side
Fears and doubts
Will run and hide
It's you and I
Our flag unfurled
Unafraid
We face the world

Adventure

Stars in your eyes
Wind in your hair
Your life's adventure
You want me there

Tailwinds are blowing
We're picking up speed
I'll give you everything
It's all that you need

Appetite

My hungry eyes
Graze upon your visage
Your sweet smile lures me in
Your curls are a waterfall
Cascading down your neck
And pooling below your chin
The portals of your eyes
Take me on a journey
Across the galaxies within
Together we travel the cosmos
To the edge of the universe
And back again
In the time it takes for me
To close my hungry eyes
Touch your soul
And breathe you in

Transcendence

Memories of a touch I've never had
Clear as crystal in my mind
Fevered hands, groping, searching
Writhing bodies will they find

Thinking of lips I've never kissed
Soft and sweet and lipstick bound
Never touched but sorely missed
In my fantasies they are found

Away in space our souls collide
Linking us forever in time
A thousand lifetimes cannot hide
That I am yours and you are mine

I understand now why I know
Your body's rhythm and your body's rhyme
We've lived and loved through ages now
These memories follow us through all time

Overcome

You've said you love me
And I've had no doubt
But seeing it, feeling it
I wasn't prepared
Like looking at the sun
The intensity was blinding
I was overcome
I openly wept for the joy
Had no other escape
From a body filled with you

Circular

My need for you
Is fed by your need for me
Is fed by my need for you
A perpetual motion machine
A perfect circle
No ending, no beginning
Just us in a bond
That is constant and unbreakable

Breathless

You take my breath

Every time I see you

But it's not until we're apart

That I can't breathe

Ensconced

I'll wrap you in my prose

Until I can wrap you in my arms

And I'll never let go with either one.

Reborn

How did my sun shine
Before it knew you?
Before it saw your eyes
How was my sky blue?
How did my heart beat
Before you gave it reason to?
How was there life on earth
Before our love grew?
So many things, my dove
That I thought I knew
Have been changed by our love
So that now everything is beautiful
And new

Moonglow

I stare at the moon through my window
A world away she looks at the same glowing orb
We both drift off, slumber taking us
To the place where our souls sleep

Fate

I never saw the hand of Fate
Until the day that I saw you
I've seen the difference it makes
When we found our purpose true
I know how long it takes
We've spent years wandering through
To find our fated mate
There's nothing we wouldn't do
In the end we followed the thread
That connected me to you

Fallen

You asked me not to fall
Like a fool I agreed
Then you grabbed me
And jumped into the void
Not knowing I never had a choice
And had fallen long ago

Giving

I want to give you
A thousand thousand kisses
And more if time permits
A lifetime of hugs and cuddles
And all our greatest hits
Spontaneous smiles
Butterflies galore
Yearnings and urges
When I walk through the door
All my love
A song to sing
My soul is yours
I'll give you everything
A happy sigh
Your smiling face
My heart is home
Within your grace

Claimed

We've claimed each other
But that doesn't mean
I get to do whatever I want to do
It means that with your consent
I get to do everything you want me to

Signals

I can tell by the way
Your ragged breath
Makes your chest heave
By the way your pulse
Shows in your throat
By the way your hips
Slowly grind against the bed
My words have worked magic
Both on your body
And inside your head

Gods

The day we met
Was the day I knew
That gods exist
Because they made you

Benevolence and mercy
Bestowed on us that day
Our love it was unleashed
And we'd never be the same

They waited until we were ready
Until they knew the time was right
So we would fall together
And love with all our might

Starmap

I never saw the hand of Fate
Until the day that I saw you
I've seen the difference it makes
When we found our purpose true
I know how long it takes
We've spent years wandering through
To find our fated mate
There's nothing we wouldn't do
In the end we followed the thread
That connected me to you

Wondrous

She has worlds in her mind

Galaxies In her eyes

Her lips, an oasis

A universe between her thighs

Her skin is electric

Her voice the ocean's swell

Her arms are a homecoming

It's only natural that I fell

Perfection

Counting things from A to Z

You're everything you need to be

You're strong, you're sweet

You're smart and true

Your inner glow, your outer hue

There's nothing more I need to see

You're completely perfect to me

I only hope that all I do

Is just as perfectly suited to you

Promise

I wish a broken clock could stop time
I'd smash them all, yours and mine
And hold us forever in that moment
Where everything was perfectly fine
But time marches without mercy
Or care about how the future's found
The only thing I can promise, love
Is I will never let you down

Anticipation

It starts with a look, or a touch

Innocent, playful

But the butterflies hit

And we both know where it's going

I love building the anticipation

Desire piling on top of desire

You love seeing where I'll take you

Before the weight becomes too much

And we crash down on each other

Gifts

The sound of your heart
The tease of your fingertips on my skin
The whisper of your breath
The brilliance of your smile
The magic of your time
The warm caress of your trust
The perfection that is you

The things that matter most
Are given but never bought
Earned but never owned

Fearless

Dancing to music only we can hear
Touching places only we can feel
Loving and laughing without fear
Bound together by magnetic appeal

Pleasure

A writhe
A moan
A gasp
A groan
Little things
Say so much
How you react
To my touch
A cry
A shake
A thrust
A quake
Pleasure found
A mutual kind
Our physical love
Begins in the mind

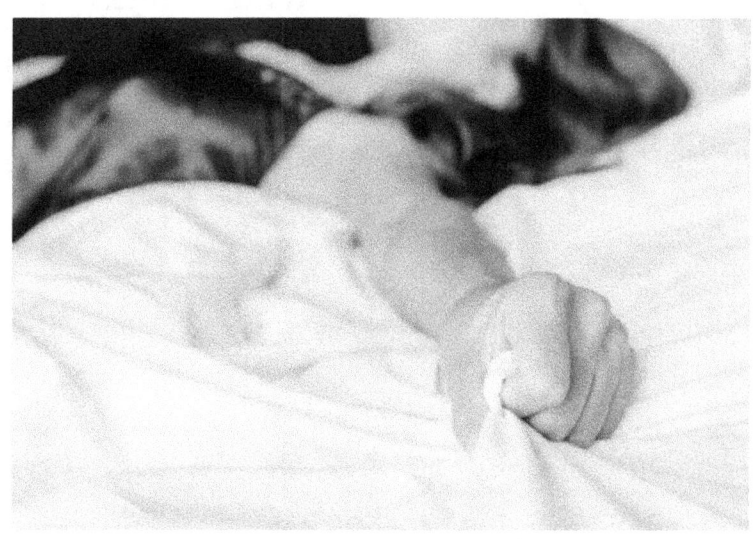

Adored

Wants

She calls me evil
With a smirk on her face
Daring me to live up to it
And praying that I do

Hellbound

I'll go through hell to get you to heaven
I'll fight for you with my heart and soul
I'll chase your demons twenty-four-seven
I'll cut out my heart to make yours whole

Wishes

Making a wish
Is a waste of time
Unless of course
That wish is mine
For I know, my love
That wishes come true
Because I closed my eyes
And I wished for you

Perfection

Your voice is a symphony

Your lips are a feast

Your curves are a sonnet

You're the beauty to my beast

My hands are explorers

Seeking new lands

Your body's an oasis

Among desert sands

You mind is a goddess

New worlds create

I kneel in her presence

Brought here by Fate

I stand in wonder

Of your celestial view

A perfect creation

And I love all of you

Patience

I am broken
You said

I can't fix you
But I'll hold your pieces together
Until you heal

I've been told I'm too much
You said

By people who weren't enough
And lacked the courage
To admit it

What did I do to deserve you?
You asked

You waded through the others
To find me, waiting,
Not for a woman
As perfect
As you
But for you
Exactly

Preference

I've been around the world
I've done a lot of things
One lesson that I've learned
So full of truth it rings
There's nothing I'd rather see
There's nothing I'd rather do
Than see your face shining bright
And spend my days loving you

Together

In my dreams you hold me tight
Pressed against me through the night
Head on chest, leg over mine
My sweet baby for all time

When I wake, you're far away
But in my mind so close you stay
Though I can't kiss those lips
You're within reach of these fingertips

Text or phone, chat or voice
Whichever's convenient is our choice
Our love is strong, it's plain to see
For I am yours and you belong to me

Stormfront

You're never alone
When you're in pain
Whatever you're feeling
I feel the same
When things get rough
And your heart aches
When skies darken
And your soul shakes
When you face the darkness
I'll stay with you
For what you're feeling
I feel it too
I'll hold your hand
Through cry and moan
No matter what
You're not alone
And when this storm ends
As they always do
I'll be right here
Next to you
My arms around you
Hand holding hand
I'm forever your friend
Your lover, your man

Only

One hand on the small of your back, pulling you tight
The other lost in your tresses, fist closed on curls
Lips joined
Tongues dancing
Your hands on the sides of my face
Breathless
Hearts pounding
The only thing that exists for me
Is you

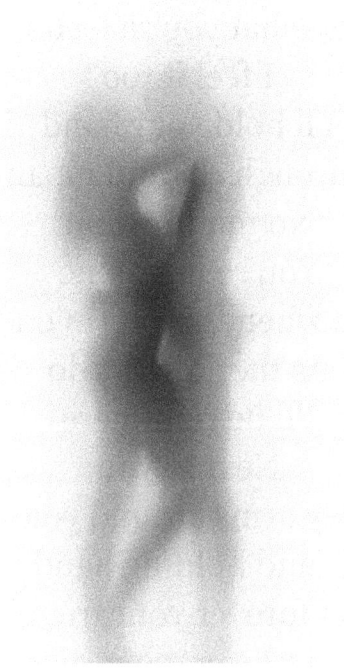

Shield

I want to breathe you in
And hold you there forever
Within me, where I know you're safe
And nothing can hurt you
Without going through me first

Impact

      Your kiss
Unlocked a door in my mind
Showing me a new world
Filled with color and song
And set my blood on fire
      Your touch
Brought me back to life
From suspended animation
A new land before me
Ready to be explored
      Your voice
Shames the great composers
A perfect symphony
Resonating with the cosmos
And calling angels home
      You
Clarified my purpose
Bringing meaning to each day
Cultivating happiness and joy
And showed me the meaning of love

Completion

Tell me you love me
As only you can
With looks and smiles
And words well planned
Soothe my soul
By loving me so
By grabbing my mind
And holding it close
Call me your baby
Make me your own
You be my queen
Poised on her throne
Complete me, my love
And make my half whole
I give you my heart
Mind, body and soul

Totality

You are my passion
Animating my soul
Giving me reason
Making me whole

You are my desire
Fueling temptation
Igniting my blood
Primal sensation

You are my purpose
Sent from above
My sacred goddess
Worshipped with love

You are my everything
So worthy and true
All that I have
I put into you

Fate

There was never a choice
Fate knew what we needed
The only question was when
Too soon and I wouldn't
Have been ready for you
Putting the egg before the hen
Too late and the moment
Would have passed us by
Where would we be then?
Fate knew the story
Written with red thread
Like we write in pen
Her timing was perfect
Her plan was exact
Balanced on the head of a pin
But she's matched us before
And in our lives yet to come
She's determined do it again

Smiles

I lay my head down
Upon my face a smile
For in my dreams I hold you
If for just a while

When I wake, you're vapor
Miles away in space
But in my heart I feel you
Hence the smile upon my face

Unknowing

She says you're her worst mistake
But how can that be
What she doesn't know
What she can't see
Is you're the best thing
To happen to me
She hates herself
And takes it out on you
She could see how amazing
You were as you grew
What she didn't know
What she couldn't see
Is that you would become
What she'd never be
Loving and caring
And strong of heart
All things she lacked
Right from the start
What she'll never know
What she'll never see
Is how very perfect
You are to me

Comparison

What's it like for you?
From raising your head
Until resting it again
Do I fill you with visions
Of joy and love and sin?
Do you see me
In the sky, the trees
Do you thank fate
And fall to your knees?
Do you breathe me in
And hold me inside
Heart pounding
Eyes open wide
If you find me in all
You touch and see
That's how loving you
Feels to me

Daybreak

Dawn brings a new day
But mine doesn't start
Until your first hello
No rooster's crow
Or alarm clock's ring
Makes my heart beat
The way your voice sings

Dreamland

I wake in the night
Thinking of you
Wondering if
You're awake too
We're connected
In a magical way
So it wouldn't surprise me
If you're also awake
Laying in bed
Waiting for sleep
Tossing and turning
Thinking of me
As I drift back toward sleep
To dream of you
I hope you share it
And dream of me too
Holding your hand
Head on your heart
Not even sleep
Can keep us apart

Blooms

She blooms like a flower
Do others see?
Or it is possible
She blooms just for me?
I know that the world
Can see her glow
She lights up the heavens
And the skyline below
But they don't know why
She lights up the land
They bask in her brilliance
But don't understand
They don't ask the questions
And they'll never know
How hard it can be
To let her bloom show
She's a warrior goddess
Strong, brave and sure
But even a goddess
Needs love that's pure
She needs support
Unconditionally
I offer it all
And I'll never leave
She ignited my blood
With her touch so demure
And everything after
Belongs just to her
My own flower's bloom
Would never occur
Without all her love
So it's just for her
She blooms like a flower
And she lets me see
That some of her beauty
She holds just for me

Sunshine

She is lightning
Creating beauty in the storm
She is Thunder
Roaring against the dark
She is rainfall
Tears falling unbidden
She is sunrise
Always pushing back my night
She is the midday sun
Making everything alright

Forever

Forever meant nothing
A concept abstract
All life is finite
No one leaves intact

Fate came along
Introduced me to you
Suddenly I get it
I know you do too

Our souls are connected
Since the dawn of time
And for all lives to come
I'm yours, you're mine

I can see to forever
And I know what to do
Each life to come
I'll be spending with you

Lucky

She tells me she's lucky

But how can that be?

I get to love her

And she loves me

I tuck her in

With good night's kiss

I wake to her face

Swaddled in bliss

Her words lift my heart

And her voice makes me smile

Her touch is a comfort

And drives me wild

She says she's lucky

Oh! Now I can see

Since she feels this too

She's as lucky as me

Strength

When storm clouds gather
You seek safety in me
When fires rage
You pull me out to sea
When nightmares strike
You make them flee
A stronger pair
There will never be
Than me for you
And you for me

Unbound

Unconditional is my love
No quid pro quo
No if this, then that
A simple statement, firm and true
Three words, eight letters
I love you

Unlimited is my love
Every day I fall a little deeper
Every day I love you more
Fate planted the seed from which it grew
It's an expanding universe
This love I have for you

Eternal is our love
The rest of this life
And all yet to come
Peaks and valleys, ascents and drops
We're worth every second
Our love never stops

Pathways

Every broken heart
Had a happy beginning
Every scar
A lesson learned
Every losing bet
Had thoughts of winning
Every bad decision
A bridge is burned

Every choice
Has led to this
The good, the bad
The black and blue
The winding pathways
Each narrow miss
It's all been worth it
For it led to you

Duality

I'll kiss you soft and tender

Love dripping from my lips

I'll map your world with my touch

Delicate skin under fingertips

I'll grab you rough and forceful

Taking what you know is mine

You desire the man and the beast

Each in his place and time

Yours

I am
That hot breath
Raising goosebumps on your flesh
I am
That soft touch
That makes you mad with desire
I am
The whispered need
That makes your heart beat fast
I am
The thrill you feel
When you think of me in the night
I am
The smile you can't hide
When you know this love is real
I am
Forevermore
Yours

Journey

Your priceless beauty
Your warrior's heart
Your glowing soul
Set you apart
Voice of an angel
At least to me
You're so much more
Than what I can see
I'll spend a lifetime
Learning about you
All of your thoughts
All that you do
Our love is a journey
An adventure so grand
Across the universe
Hand in hand
We're in this together
It's always we two
And there's no one I'd rather
Be with than you

Eternal

This heart has always belonged to you
Before the earth had sea and land
When our souls were roaming space
It's always had I t proper place
This loving heart's been in your hands

This heart may beat inside my chest
But it's you that it's beating for
I think of you and It starts to race
A smile spreads across my face
And every day I love you more

Moods

Some days are lovely
And all goes right
Some days are moody
Dark as the pitch of night
It doesn't matter
My day or my mood
Always I love you
Even if I brood
For moods are fleeting
And bad days end
But always I love you
My woman, my friend
The light that you give me
Cures any bad day
And through any you suffer
At your side I'll stay
Life isn't easy
It's often a chore
But our love conquers all
And will evermore

Knowing

You'll know
By the intensity in my eyes
As I drink you in
By the growl in my throat
As I touch your skin
By the way my muscles flex
As I hold you tight
By the way my heart pounds
As we give in to the night
By the way that our souls merge
As they were always meant to be
You'll know that nothing will matter
Like you matter to me

New

You're the first arc of sun
In a breaking dawn
The first hint of color
In a springtime lawn
My first thought in the morning
Before I open my eyes
The first drops of rain
From warm summer skies
You're everything perfect
Beautiful and new
I am reborn every day
I spend loving you

Decisions

I wake in the night
Thoughts of you
Burning bright
Do I rise?
Turn on the light?
Conjure you
In my sight
Or close my eyes
Dreams taking flight
Holding you close
Feeling delight
Either one
Will solve my plight
My life with you
Feels so right
Loving each other
With all our might

Senses

I breathed you in
And now my lungs are empty
When you're not near
I saw your face
And now I'm blinded
To everything but you
I heard your voice
Rendering me deaf
To all but your song
I touched your soul
And learned how it feels
To be bathed in love

Stability

Your soul quiets my mind
When it's buzzing and pulling me down
When I start to spiral
Your words put me on solid ground
As much as I am your rock
The stable shore on which you lean
It works both ways, my darling
And you'll never know how much that means

Whole

She wants his touch
Gentle. Rough. Spoons in bed.
She just wants to feel him against her.
She want to hold his heart in her hands
And show him she'll take care of it

He wants to give himself to her.
Hold her close, keep her warm. Safe.
When his heart beats
The same tune as hers
He knows he can trust her with it

Separate they are want and need
Together they are friction and fire
Separate they are halves of wholes
Together they are love entire

Connected

Across the dark
Eyes spring open
Fumbling hands
Reach for you
And find you there
Awake, alert
Reaching back
Connection made
Sparks ignite
Rumbling heartbeats
Minds spring open
Across the dark

Cravings

I crave
Your face in the morning light
Your voice in my ear at night
Your stories, hopes and fears
Your desires as my love draws near
Your delicate hand, your lover's touch
No amount of you can be too much
Where you go, my love is found
To your fate, mine is bound
I crave you, my love
Entire, whole
I crave your mind, your body
Your heart, and soul

Changes

Since I met you
Nothing is the same
Have you changed my world
Or just changed me
Have you changed my world
Or just the way I see
Have you changed my world
Or just the way I feel
Have you changed my world
Or can it be real
That nothing is the same
Since I met you

Needs

Everything I need is in
The touch of your fingers on mine
Your breath on my chest
My lips on your neck
Your voice in my ear
Telling me it will be okay
Everything I need is in
Being open and vulnerable
Trusting you with my heart and soul
Knowing you got me
Everything I need is in
Holding you against me
Feeling you relax
Knowing you trust me to protect your heart
I don't need much
Just all of you
Forever

Awakenings

When I wake and reach for you
I wonder if you do that too
Do you feel me where you are
Pressed against you, wrapped in my arms?
I feel you here, next to me
You body soft, your spirit free
Your beating heart, your breath so sweet
No gap between us from head to feet
My waking mind plays tricks on me
You disappear despite my plea
But I close my eyes and there you are
My shining love, my guiding star
And so it is, I know, for you
When you wake, your slumber through
That though my body is far away
You close your eyes, and with you I'll stay

Rewarding

Your name on my lips
Is an addiction
Your hand in mine
Slows down time
Intimate moments
Sweetest friction
Your head on my chest
So sublime
Our souls twined together
Is perfection
Hearts beating as one
Strikes a chord
Bodies bound to each other
Fate's selection
A lifetime's love
Our reward

Transformed

There comes a time
When you join a cause
Something bigger than you
In which you get lost
Sometimes it's noble
Sometimes it's fun
But it so consumes you
You've nowhere to run
We fell for each other
Heart traded for heart
We're greater together
Than we are apart
I'm so very happy
It fills me with glee
That the beginning of us
Was the ending of me

Pairs

Your mind and voice
Captured my heart
I had no choice

Your laugh and smile
Sped up my fall
It was so worthwhile

Your love and care
Made my life
Easy to bear

Your heart and soul
Perfectly fit
And made me whole

Resolute

I wish I had a thousand years to tell you
All the things that make me swoon
All the things that you do to me
That make my heart soar wild and free
All the things you say and do
Strike my heart with aim most true
And leave my words silent and mute
So I must be more resolute
I'll write for you what's in my heart
When my voice fails on emotion's part
Black with ink and wet with tears
I'll write for you my remaining years

Reclaimed

Hands on your shoulders
Lips on your neck
I'm getting bolder
You're getting wet
Hips rocking forward
Legs open wide
A gasp and moan
You take me inside
Pounding with pleasure
Grinding with glee
Howling like beasts
Wild and free
Eyes on each other
Our tremors start
Losing control now
Breaking apart
Sated and blissful
It's easy to see
I'm claimed by you, love
And you're claimed by me

Lost

I get lost in a good movie
Or in a really good book
I feel the emotions
And away I am took
For a little while
I cease to be
I become a character
On page or screen
I must be well written
I know you are too
For each day I get lost
In the pages of you

Could

I could write a million words
And never cover how I feel
I could conquer all the world
And show a fraction of my zeal
I could move heaven and earth
The laws of physics I'll repeal
Then I could bend time and space
To relive our love's reveal
Instead I'll take each day anew
And highlight all of your appeal
Every moment, word and action true
And show you that this love is real

Lifesaver

When life gets rough
I think first of you
You give me strength
To make it through
Your hand in mine
Through the night
I see your face
My guiding light
You fit my life
Hand in glove
My safe home
My one true love

Evermore

You have my sword
My life is yours
In deed and word
You never need ask
You plea is heard
Our fate is bound
In love and war
Through lakes of fire
To burning shore
Our exploits become
The stuff of lore
And my love for you is
Evermore

Magic

I say you're magical
And you say you're just you
But you don't understand
Just what you can do
The weight of the world
Stress, worry, and fear
One word from you
And it all disappears
Part of your magic
It seems to me
Is the outsized effect
Of your love on me
I don't know for certain
But I hope it's true
That my love is magic
When I give it to you

Adored

Light

You're the last ember in my daytime sky
The first star to appear at night
Your light never leaves me
And I'll never stop giving it a place to shine.

Deserving

When you say I'm good to you
And I'm just doing things I think are normal
I realize you're not used to hearing that
You're magical
Wonderful
Brilliant
Beautiful
Sexy
As much as that makes me
Sad, angry for your past
It reminds me that Fate paired us
And I know we were put together
Because I have so much love to give
And you deserve it all
Every day
Forever

Comfort

It's you I reach for
When I wake at night
Weary from the storm
Seeking your body
Pulling you tight
Skin so warm

In the dark night
When you awake
With nightmare's sight
For your mind's
To ease your fright
My hand you take

Though far apart
We're connected
From the start
We each selected
The other's heart
A love perfected

Pain

It's impossible to sleep
When I know you're in pain
And I can do nothing to
Take it away
I feel you across the miles
Wrap you in my arms
And hold you so you know
You're not alone
It isn't much, I know
But what else can i do?
When you're in pain, love
I feel it too

Scribe

I'll write for you our story
Until my pen runs dry
Then I'll use a quill
Pierce a vein
And give another try
When the quill's nib breaks
And my blood won't flow
I'll etch it a in a stone
Nothing will stop our story, love
We'll never stand alone
When my tools grow dull
And the stone won't etch
I'll carve it in my skin
And proclaim my love
For you my dear
Over and over again

Suspended

When we sleep and our thoughts go
To the dark side of the moon
Waking always feels like
Emerging from a cocoon
Where did the time go?
How much has passed?
Like suspended animation
It goes by so fast
When I wake in the morning
My first thought is of you
My goddess, my love, my angel
The one who gets me through
My first words each day
Are for your ears alone
Good morning, beautiful
My queen upon her throne

POV

If you felt how I feel
When I see you
If you saw what I see
When I think of you
If you could have my eyes
My mind
My heart
For just one moment
You'd know
How wonderfully consumed
I am by your fire

Hunted

The curve of your hip
The pout of your lip
The lust in your eye
Your soft inner thigh
Passionate kiss
Sweet, dewy bliss
The scent of desire
Seeping from your pores
Enticing me, luring me
And making me yours

Adored

Linguist

I will weave words in infinite combinations

To show you the unlimited nature of my love

Location

There is nowhere on earth
That I'd rather be
Than the place and the moment
Where it's you and me
It matters not
What we say or do
The important thing
Is I'm next to you
Reading a book
Watching TV
Random chatting
Folding laundry
I crave your opinions
And your virtual touch
24/7
Can't be too much
I've fallen for you
A blind man could see
To put it quite simply
You're perfect to me
Through every day
Good times, and rough
When it comes to you, love
I can't get enough

Magical

There's magic in you
I can't explain
You give me strength
When I feel pain
You make my heart race
From miles away
You add meaning to life
Every day
We feel connected
As we lay in bed
You hear my heartbeat
Where you lay your head
There's magic in you
It's plain to see
And you've activated
The magic in me

Guardian

Lost in the wilderness
I see your face in the moon
Leading me to safety
Lost at sea
Your voice in the waves
Makes me swoon
And brings me to shore
There's no place on earth
Where you can't reach me
Touch me
Calm me
Bring me peace
And guide me
Home to you

Guidance

She is my midnight sky
Always there
Even when I can't see her

She is my magnetic north
Guiding me
When I'm lost at sea

She is my shooting star
Blazing bright
All my wishes come true

Vocal

Your words touch me
In places unseen
Reserved just for you
My beautiful queen
They stroke my skin
And bring me to heel
They steal my breath
Their impact is real
The range of emotions
They bring out of me
They move me to tears
Or I laugh with glee
With every letter
My heart beats so fast
I hang on each word
Like it could be the last
Your words, they touch me
So loving and kind
They stroke my skin
And make love to my mind

Beautiful

A thousand types of beauty

Swirl through your veins

From your face so soft and perfect

To your world building brains

Your choice of nail polish

The cereal you eat

The clothes upon your body

The shoes upon your feet

The way you call me baby

Cooing like a dove

Our cuddles in the morning

The way you wear my love

A thousand types of beauty

Wondrous, pure, large and small

And for rest of our lives together

I'm going to list them all

If

If only I could hold you
If only I were there
If only you were in my lap
And I were playing with your hair
If only I could touch you
If only we could kiss
If only I could call your name
When falling into bliss
If only doesn't matter
When I love you like I do
We're so connected, you and I
That I get all of you
I feel you in my lap
I get to touch your hair
I get to kiss your lips, my love
As if I'm really there
I get to say good morning
I get to tuck you in
I get to call your name out loud
When we're lost within our sin
We get to be together
With help from Fate above
You fill my life with so much joy
And never ending love

Bare

When you bare your soul to me
It's an honor that I love
When you show me all your flaws
I swear to the gods above
Everything you show me
Fits me like a glove
There's nothing you can share
That will ever scare me away
Your darkest fears and issues
Give me more reason to stay
Your pieces paint a picture
That only I can see
A masterpiece in motion
You've revealed just to me
You're perfect as you are, love
From your surface to your core
For each piece that you reveal
I only love you more

Bedtime

Ten thousand times
I'll tuck you in
And sleep right by your side
Ten thousand times
We'll cuddle close
And I'll hold you through night
Ten thousand times
When you wake up
I'll have three words for you
Ten thousand times
No matter what
Good morning beautiful
Ten thousand times
Then ten thousand more
And on through the end of time
I'll hold you tight
And love you true
Ever grateful you are mine

Homeward

Always in the dark
My mind turns its eye to you
As I drift away, dreaming now
You're never far from my view
In dreams I try to take control
But the mind doesn't work that way
Tangled roads in strange dreamscapes
Try to lead me astray
But always love, in dreams and life
I know just what to do
It's simple really, I'll choose the path
That leads me home to you

Worthwhile

If I could pick and choose
The best moments of my life
Would I pick the easy ones?
Free of hurt and strife?
Or would I choose the hard won fights
Where my will did persevere?
Should adversity overcome
Be what is most revered?
No, the proudest moments of my life
The ones most worth their while
Are every single time, my love
That I have made you smile

Counting

If I tried to count the things
I love about you
From dawn to dusk, counting
Is all I'd ever do
I'm consumed by your fire
And bathed in your light
I run with your wild
And lose my breath at your sight
My first thought on waking
My last thought at night
My guiding star
A beacon so bright
Each moment together
Is unbridled bliss
But the thing I love most
Is you let me love you like this

Promises

Your eyes promise

Adventure

Like I've never known

Mystery

I'm invited to solve

Passion

I feel in my soul

Seduction

Luring me like the siren's song

Love

To sustain me for a thousand years

Your eyes make the promise

Your mind writes the script

Together we make it real

Timeless

All time is relative
That is a certain fact
Hard times last forever
Good times go so fast
Then there's time spent with you
Each moment a sweet lifetime
Yet weeks and months go flying by
Stolen in life's greatest crime
Time believes it gets to flow
With no regard for what we want
Our love will last forever, though
So hand in hand, it's time we taunt

Bliss

Small desires
Tiny fires
Grow in force
And form a pyre
Mad with lust
Your brain or bust
I want you all
Our love I trust
Our lover's dream
No greater thing
We're twined as one
A perfect team
We never miss
Due to Fate's kiss
A thousand lives
With you is bliss

Symphonic

You're lyrical
A magical song which never ends
But takes me through crescendo and resolution
Wave and crash, foreplay and climax
Over and over
And the music never ends

Companions

From the day that we met
My lonely days were through
No matter the time or place
My mind is filled with you
You're with me in my waking hours
Next to me while I sleep
We're bound together soul to soul
My heart is yours to keep
I see you in the morning sun
I hear you in the blackbird's song
I feel you in the wind's caress
You're always with me all day long
It's not a revelation
I know it's nothing new
For when you reach your hand for mine
I'm always there for you

Two

There's only one sun
Keeping our planet alive
Only one moon
Making the oceans thrive
Only one galaxy
In which we reside
Only one universe
Through which we glide
There are trillions of stars
In the black of night
But we just need ours
For our life's delight
There are billions of people
On this this rock we know
Basking in warm light
Or the moon's soft glow
Our universe is reduced
To one sun and one moon
And for our perfect life
There's just me and you

Ask

There's nothing you can ask
That I won't do for you
You can talk about your problems
Until your face is blue
You can lay your head
Upon my chest
Every time
You need a rest
I'll hold you close
Through every night
And of course I'll do
That thing you like
I'll hold your hand
I'll cook and clean
I'll wash the clothes
Run the vacuum machine
There nothing I won't do for you
Nothing feels like a task
We're partners, love, in all of life
You never even need to ask

Scars

Every scar tells a story
Some funny, some sad
Some scars long healed
And some drive us mad
I want to see yours
Don't hide them from view
Your scars and your story
Are what led me to you
I treasure each mark
On your soul and your skin
For the stories that made them
Led to where we begin
Our pasts are over
They can't be undone
But the future is ours, love
Together as one

2AM

It's 2 am and I'm thinking of you
It's no surprise because I always do
It's only because I love you true
And I know you love me too

I know because you think of me
More time together your only plea
You close your eyes, my face you see
At 2 am it's my touch you need

Fate has gifted us a world of bliss
Where not just our bodies, but our souls kiss
The moment we part, the other we miss
For there's never been a love like this

Needs

I have a need
To tell you all the things
Whether whispered sweetly
In your ear
Or broadcast for the world
To hear
You're brilliant, talented,
Hyper observant
Gorgeous, exciting
A love most fervent
Playful, loving
Stealer of breath
I'll continue to praise you
Until the moment of death
I have a need
To let you know
I'll love you forever
Mind, Body, and soul

Curves

The curves of your body
Are magic to me
My fingers can wander
Where only we see
You can wiggle so close
As we cuddle at night
My arms wrapped around you
You fit me just right
But it's your mind that seduces
And draws me in
Loving me sweetly
While begging for sin
The curves of your body
Are magic to me
But it's your mind, my sweet baby
That sets my love free

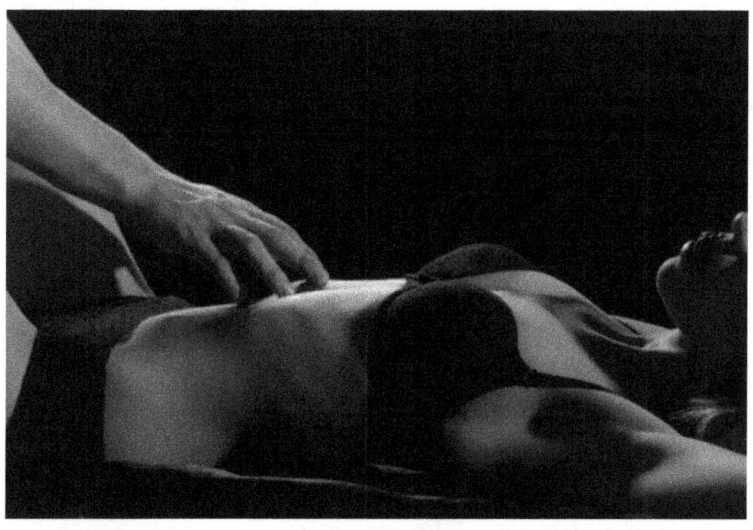

Inheritance

Fortune favors the bold
But the meek shall inherit the earth
Maybe it's a mix of both
That helps determine one's worth
It was a bold move
The way we first met
Not one I planned on
But the most consequential yet
Yet I'm meek enough to know
Just how lucky I am
To have been included
In Fate's master plan
Each day that passes
I'll keep proving my worth
For you are my world, love
And the meek shall inherit this earth

Power

"I love you"

The most powerful three words

In the English language.

Time stops

Distance disappears

Hearts beat faster

Moods get better

The stars line up for you

The moon winks at you,

Knowing you've been given fuel

To make your soul glow as brightly as it does

Bricks

I built my walls
Brick by hard earned brick
High enough to protect my heart
And half again as thick
I was prepared to live my life
Isolated, alone
Prepared to make this space
My everlasting home
I never expected you
With your eyes so blue
And smile so bright
To pass right through
It's as if for you
These walls didn't exist
You grabbed my heart
And I couldn't resist
But the best part of this
Was right from the start
You lowered your walls
And gave me your heart
Hand in hand
Safe from attack
We fell in love
And never looked back

20/20

In your eyes
Exists every universe
In which our love exists
Every scenario played out
In some, we're together
From the start
In others we meet
In a bar
In a store
At a stoplight
And sparks fly
But thanks to fate
In all of them
We end up the same
We love each other
Forever
And I can see it all
In your eyes

Matched

Hearts on fire

Burning desire

Want and need

From our souls bleed

Our claims are just

In love we trust

Passions cried

Cannot hide

Always sure

Love so pure

We adore

Evermore

Worthy

My heart knew
The moment we met
That you were the one
On you it was set
My love is a treasure
Securely locked away
Until someone deserves it
There it will stay
Like the sword in the stone
My love was meant for you
You had but to claim it
If you only wanted to
Of course you were worthy
As Fate knew you'd be
For what can't be stolen
I gave you for free

Artwork

Your skin is the canvas upon which I want to paint my desires.
Your mind is the palette from which I'll draw the tint.

Conception

I see your face in the stars

Where the gods conceived your beauty

I hear your voice in the wind

Where they took the melody to make you sing

I feel your hand on my heart

Where you placed it when I opened myself to you

I feel your soul on mine

Where it belongs until the end of time

Steadfast

I'm soaked in your storm
Steadfast and sure
Drowning in emotion
Dangers inured
Full steam ahead
Compass aligned
It's you I desire
Destiny resigned
Single of purpose
Steadfast and true
My mission is certain
I'm sailing for you

Intimacy

I let her gaze upon my naked form
But that was just a look

I let her feel my exposed body
But that was just a touch

I let her into my heart
But those are just feelings

When I let her into my mind
Then, oh then, we were intimate

Return

I thought I was ready to give her my heart
The truth was, my heart had always been hers, even before I knew her.
I simply returned it to where it was meant to be

Doubtless

With you I'm fearless
I'll jump into the void
No look, no worry
Doubts are destroyed
With you at my side
I can't be stopped
You give me strength
To come out on top
It goes both ways
This life with no fear
You're strong without me
That much is clear
But with me beside you
You have help on demand
All you need to do
Is reach for my hand

Amnesia

I can't remember what life was like
Before you came along
And what's more, I don't want to

Strong

There's a strength in you
That some might miss
You rise to the occasion
For family and friends
You're so strong for others
It's just what you do
So I have the need, love
To be strong for you

Missing

I miss you
The moment we part
Whether for work
Or sleep in the dark
Your voice, your words
Your beautiful face
The feel of your touch
The warmth of your grace
The blue of your eyes
The curls in your hair
The polish on your nails
The way that you care
The look when you say
That you love me too
I miss each tiny thing
That reminds me of you
Counting the seconds
Can be pretty rough
Too much of you, woman
Is still not enough

Mine

How can I see you
And not turn you into poetry

How can I hear you
And not sing your name

How can I know you
And not fall in love

You are my passion
You are my desire
You are my fate

You are mine

Heartbeat

Lay your head on my chest and listen to my heart.
Drift to sleep knowing that it beats for you

Smiles

I can't stop smiling
When I think of you
Morning, noon, and night
The whole day through
I smile when I see your face
Your lips, your eyes
My saving grace
I smile when you message me
My phone will buzz
Giving me glee
I smile when we sleep at night
Arms around you
Held so tight
It's not a matter of what we do
That keeps my grin fixed in place
As long as I can love you true
You'll see a smile upon my face

Enmeshed

Your body pressed against mine
Soft curves fitting my hard angles
Your pliant flesh, sweet and yielding
Cleaved to me
This is my desire
This is my dream

Kiss

To kiss your lips
Is the reward of a lifetime
To feel their pliant flesh
Pressed to mine
Completing a circuit
Letting passion flow
Instead of electricity
Fire down below
A thousand fantasies
Pass between
Each hungry for more
Desire unseen
Yearning
Wanting
Needing
Demanding
Searching
Pleading
The galaxy shifts
Around the gravity
Of your kiss

Priceless

What is the value of a single word?
It brings a world of beauty
Passion
Desire
Boundless hope
Inner fire
It lifts me up to the sky
Looping
Soaring
Wings unfurled
Pleasure roaring
It brings me peace
Tranquil
Serene
Calming seas
Beauty seen
What is this word
How much can it do
I'll learn in time
For that word
Is YOU

Verbiage

I only have my words to hold you with

They need to be as strong as my arms

As warm as my heart

And as soft as my soul

But they're yours, always yours.

Darkness

In the dark of night
You're most alone
Your mind retreats
To your safe home
Inside my heart
Which beats for you
Forever yours
This love so true

In the dark of night
I'm most alone
Across the void
Is my safe home
Inside your heart
Is where I'll be
There you give
You love to me

Sleep

There's a disturbance
Felt in the night
Are you okay
Or dealing with fright
Barely awake
Or dreaming now
I know you're safe
I wipe my brow
When I wake in the night
For reasons unknown
I'm connected to you
History has shown
We're there for each other
Through nightmares and pain
Our souls connected
Nights never the same
All that I know
Whatever we do
There's nothing better
Than sleeping with you

Alternates

In a parallel universe
Things are not the same
Life is better there
They often make the claim
On another planet
In a universe parallel
The grass isn't any greener
And here's how I can tell
No matter the circumstance
No matter what we do
Fate has mapped it out
So that I get to be with you
There's no greater joy
That can ever be had
Than being at your side
In this or other lands
So our alternate selves
Whether they're distant or near
Are only just as happy
As we are here

Knight

I'll always be there
Through the thick and the thin
You'll never wonder about me, love
With you, I am all in
I'm always at your side
I'll always have your back
You have my support without asking, love
We'll weather any attack
I trust you with my heart
I trust you with my life
I'm at your side through every day
And I got you every night
If ever you have troubles
If ever life's not fair
Just reach your hand out for mine, love
And trust that I'll be there

Ghosts

Your fingers are ghosts
Leaving trails upon my skin
I follow the goosebumps
To see where they have been
I dream about their touch
Soft, tender and light
It doesn't matter where
I've never known such delight
My craving is so intense
I'd make the devil his deal
If I could trade my dreams
And feel your touch for real

Overwatch

Did you sense me in the night?
Watching over you.
Guarding you

Did you hear me?
Whispering in your ear 'I got you.'

Did you feel me?
Loving you.
My soul twined with yours
Burning brighter than both of them separately.

I sensed you.
Heard you.
Felt you.
And it felt so right

Hope

Between the moon's glow
and her stardust smile
lay a universe of hope and beauty
laid bare for all to see

Memories

I have memories of us
Burned into my brain
Places we've never been
But we'll visit once again
I have memories of us
Happy, loving, free
Things that haven't happened
But we know someday will be
I have memories of us
Pictures in my mind
Blurry, indistinct
Lost somewhere in time
Memories are dreams
Preludes of what will be
I cherish each single one
That brings you closer to me

Apparition

As I drift off, thinking of you
You begin forming, warm, secure in my arms
I sleep content with you next to me
As I wake, you become a vapor
A wisp fading in the morning light
I open my eyes, and I am alone
But between sleep and wake, I am with you
I am whole

Inadequate

The poems I write don't do justice
To the way I see you, or feel about you
These are just words
But until you can
See yourself through my eyes
Hear my thoughts about you
Feel my heart race
Rejoice in your presence
And dread your absence
These will have to do

Romanticize

Wild hair and hungry eyes
Tender touch, butterflies
Rapid breath trembling thighs
Whispered needs and growled replies
Lover's clench and passion's rise
Heaving chest and desperate sighs
Crescendo, crash, and sweet reprise
Puddled bliss intimate prize
Forever together solidifies

Sowed

One by one she showed me
Skeletons in her closet
And secrets she held fast
They made her beauty grow
And ensured that it would last
Bit by bit she showed me
The trust she placed in me
It's nothing that she owed
I'd earned it piece by piece
Day by day she showed me
The love she had for me
And never would we part
For Fate had let her know
I was hers from the start

Unconditional

Whether drenched with the sweat of passion
Or merely thinking of you while I sleep
Living a blissful life euphoric
Or struggling our way through troubles deep
My love is for you, not the circumstance
And always you in my heart I'll keep

Patience

I would do anything
To fix your heart
Write the greatest song
Ever to chart
Put your favorite things
In an Amazon cart
Remind you each day
That you're so very smart
But the truth is nothing
Can fix your heart but time
And distance from the wound
That hurt that heart of mine
Minutes, hours, days
On the clock will chime
I'll wait with you
While you heal your heart
And eventually, love
The pain will depart
And you'll see yourself
As I have from the start
You'll look in the mirror
And see a work of art

Forever

She comes like the dawn
Fresh, new, full of promise
Every day she's revealed anew
Takes your breath
Fills your heart
Restores your soul
And you thank god
For letting you be with her
Just one more day
And tomorrow, one more
And on
And on and on
Into forever

Home

My time on this planet is divided in two.
Before we met, and after

Two worlds, a universe apart
The other seems far away
Empty
Desolate

This one is full of life
Full of light
And feels like home

Adored

My life is a piece from heaven torn
The bounty strikes my heart so true
Fresh, crisp air on an autumn morn
A brilliant sunrise and sky so blue
A love so pure I feel reborn
And a lifetime spent adoring you

Eternal

I knew your soul
Before we met
And eternal pair
The perfect set

A thousand
times
The gods above
Have placed us
here
To find our love

It may take time
But my heart is
true
In every life
I'm choosing
you

Blink

Like light traveling
Through the night sky
So much can happen
In the blink of an eye
It took just one moment
To fall hard for you
And one moment longer
You fell for me too
In that moment
I gave you my heart
You gave yours in return
So never we'd part
The blink of an eye
A moment in time
I became yours forever
And you're always mine

Radiance

She's made of stardust
An angel with gossamer wings
She brings me hope and love and lust
And so many other things

She's lit from within
By a celestial light
Radiant in virtue and sin
I love her with all my might

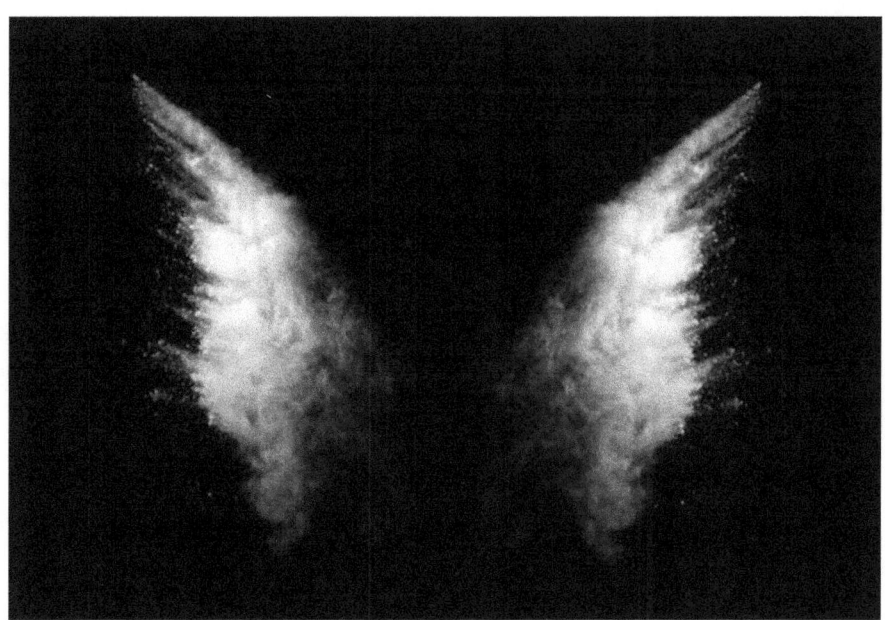

About The Author

 Hi! I'm HA Blackwood. It's a pen name, but I've grown pretty fond of it. I love the people I've met undertaking this adventure in writing erotic romance. I've made a lot of friends and we've had a lot of fun together. Don't read too much into that. Wink. I love the arid high plains desert of Colorado and enjoy exploring with the boss of me, a feisty beagle with a nose for rabbits and an insatiable love of the trail. There are more adventures planned in my little universe, some with Darcy and Gemma and some with other characters. Stick around—you'll be (hopefully) pleasantly surprised.

Other Books From H.A. Blackwood

Tell-Tale Hearts

Darcy Ford is coming off an ill-advised relationship that ended in disaster. When she's at her lowest point, she meets a woman who takes her back ten years to a night of wild passion. A night when she met-and lost-someone who opened new worlds to her. A night where her heart was stolen. A night which was the beginning of this most recent disastrous affair. Only by re-telling these tales can she find her way back to her lost love and the return of her heart.

Candid Camera

A new relationship. A secret from the past. Will their love survive?

Darcy Ford and Gemma Amante are contemplating the next big move in their relationship when Ashleigh, a lover from Gemma's past, shows up unexpectedly. She brings news that has Darcy and Gemma on a trip to Los Angeles.

Gemma's friends from her old life as a sex worker are in trouble and need help. Going undercover as sex cam workers in the city of sin may seem like a literal pleasure trip, but when they go up against a new type of criminal, they're going to need all of their sexy savvy. Between steamy escapades, clues begin to emerge. If they're going to solve this mystery, they'll have to risk their way of life, their relationship, and their very lives.

Other Books From Baying Hound Media

Still Yours
By Cara Roman

High school sweethearts, Ridge left Leigha shortly after graduation to follow his dreams of a career in the music business. Finding his success, but missing home, he is back 12 years later trying to earn a second chance with Leigha. Ridge isn't some 18-year-old teenager anymore, a lot has changed. Can Leigha open up and trust her heart to the man who broke it all those years ago?

Definitely Memorable
By Cara Roman

Caitlyn has always dreamed of vacationing in Ireland. After a disappointing divorce she decides its time she does something for herself. What she didn't count on was meeting a charming and devastatingly handsome Irishman, Nolan in a pub. Unable, or unwilling to deny the chemistry between them she throws caution to the wind embarking on a whirlwind romance. Love is never as simple as it seems though, and hers takes a course she never could have predicted.

Without A Wolf (Big Woods Pack Book One)
By Cara Roman

New in town, Emma Lowe was hiding a big secret. Wolf shifter Kian Decker needed to find out who she was, and why she was so very appealing to him. Turns out Emma wasn't the only one in town with secrets. Now their lives have been turned upside down, and they need to figure where they stand.

Running From The Wolf (Big Woods Pack Book Two)
By Cara Roman

The second book in the Big Woods Pack series, Kayla Decker spent years being mad at Lex Kolter. Using her anger as a shield to keep Lex at bay isn't working so well since the shake ups in the pack. Just when they stop fighting each other new information comes to light threatening the pack once again.